190 WILD FLOWERS OF

MOHAVE - COLORADO
WESTERN ARIZONA

Published by:

BEST-WEST PUBLICATIONS
P. O. Box 757, Palm Desert, Calif.

Design Art and Production by:

LITHO COLOR CO., ORANGE, CALIF.

THE SOUTHWEST DESERTS
IN NATURAL COLOR

BY

GRACE B. and ONAS M. WARD

580
War

To our Son

John Brodhead Ward

Preface

The purpose of this book is to stimulate interest in the Flowers of the Desert, and to aid flower lovers in identifying those pictured here. Each flower is shown with its Common, Scientific and Family name. Since we are only amateur botanists, we have depended, for identification and description material of many of the flowers, on recognized experts in the field.

The photographs are arranged according to color: Reddish, Bluish, Whitish, Yellowish, and they were taken on the Mohave, Colorado and Western Arizona Deserts, ("The Three Deserts").

There are several thousand varieties of Wild Flowers in California and Arizona, and perhaps more than fifteen hundred varieties found on The Three Deserts. Of these, less than two hundred are represented here. The various Gilias, Phacelias and Penstemons, among many, are so much alike that only the more observant and perhaps technically interested person will want to differentiate between them. The more discriminating student can turn to "A California Flora" by Munz and Keck for more detail.

Germination is determined by sufficient moisture and mild temperature. Moisture is the uncertain factor, and years may pass without enough rainfall to stimulate plant growth. Some Desert Flower seeds have water-soluble germination inhibitors in their coverings and hence fail to sprout even after rain, unless the moisture totals at least half-an-inch. Rains on the Desert are very uncertain and can be expected any time from September through April, but — they may not come at all. One year, Palm Springs had a scanty half-inch for the entire year.

We lived in, or adjacent to, the Desert for more than thirty-three years, and only once in that time did we see the Desert fully in bloom. Then, from Palm Springs to Yuma, across the Western Arizona Desert to Blythe and Needles, and through the Mohave Desert to Barstow and to San Bernardino, the entire area was a mass of colorful Wild Flowers — a sight rarely seen, and one never forgotten.

Because the Desert rains are so erratic, our colored slides have been collected over a long period of years, and many miles of Desert travel. It has been a most interesting and enjoyable experience.

A word of caution: For the greater enjoyment of your Desert Flower trip, SLOW DOWN! — Drive Slowly — Stop Often and Look! While driving at sixty miles per hour, you cannot notice detail. To get the most out of your trip, stop the car and get out — you will be amazed at what lies at your feet.

On one occasion, friends invited us on a trip to see a display of Wild Flowers that the local newspapers had rated rather high. On arrival at the area, there was no big display to be seen, but we stopped along the highway where there was a bit of color and, on closer observation, we were able to identify some thirty varieties in an area less than one hundred feet across. UNUSUAL? Perhaps, for this spot was watered by the run-off from the road. However, it is not uncommon to find ten or more varieties at almost any display of Desert Wild Flowers.

While Cactus blossoms, some of the Primroses, the Datura, Coyote Melon, Desert Lily are quite large, many of the Desert Wild Flowers are very small — some less than one-eighth of an inch in diameter. These are often referred to as "BELLY FLOWERS" for, in order to get a "close-up", one must get down to eye level.

In photographing the Desert Flowers, we have used a variety of different cameras, the Leica, Contax, Exakta among others. We strongly recommend a single lens reflex type, which permits critical focussing. Be sure you have a good lens with a pre-set semi- or automatic diaphragm arrangement. We prefer a Zeiss Biotar F2 and, using a No. 3 close-up attachment, one can work to within ten inches of the subject. If greater magnification is needed, one can switch to a No. 10 and work to within four inches.

On the Desert, there is almost always a breeze, and one must have a lot of patience and wait until there is a lull to get the desired photo. A fairly fast shutter speed can be used, but sometimes faster shutter speeds call for a larger opening of the lens aperture, and this could mean sacrificing depth of focus. But — with a little bit of luck and plenty of patience, you can obtain good color slides.

If this book gives you pleasure, or creates a desire to know more about our wonderful Desert-land, we shall feel amply repaid.

"The Wards"

Special Thanks to

Oscar Clark, *Herbarium, University of California, Riverside.*

William and "Sandy" Dengler, *Joshua Tree National Monument.*

Percy C. Everett, *Rancho Santa Ana Botanic Garden.*

Edmund C. Jaeger, *Botanist, Author.*

Gordon A. Marsh, *Curator, Museum of Systematic Biology,*
University of California, Irvine.

The Naturalist Staff, *Joshua Tree National Monument.*

For their help in identification of the flower slides.

Red Flowers
of the Desert

INDEX

Reddish Flowers

1. DESERT MALLOW
Sphaeralcea ambigua
Mallow Family
A shrubby perennial, very
showy, with flowers deep
apricot to red. All three
deserts.

2. INDIAN PAINTBRUSH
Castilleja
Figwort Family
A perennial with brilliant
red bracts and inconspicuous
flowers. All three deserts.

3. BEAVERTAIL
Opuntia basilaris
Cactus Family
Flower magenta to orchid.
The grey to purplish joints
are flat and spineless, but
bear glochids, or spicules.
Three deserts.

4. HEDGEHOG - CALICO CACTUS
Echinocereus Engelmannii
Cactus Family
Flowers dark rose or purple.
Common on all three deserts.

5. FIRECRACKER
BEARD TONGUE
Penstemon Eatonii
Figwort Family
A perennial, with scarlet
flowers on tall stems, and
smooth, dark-green leaves.
Mohave and Arizona Deserts.

6. MOHAVE ASTER
Aster abatus
Sunflower Family
Flower violet to almost
white, with yellow center.
Usually many flower heads
on a single plant. Colorado
and Mohave Deserts.

7. DESERT RATTLEWEED
Astragalus crotalariae
Davidsonii
Pea Family
Flower reddish purple.
Mohave Desert.

8. SCARLET LOCOWEED
Astragalus coccineus
Pea Family
The scarlet flowers make this one of the most vividly colored plants of the desert. Common to the Colorado and Mohave Deserts.

9. OCOTILLO
COACH-WHIP-CANDLEWOOD
Fouquieria splendens
Ocotillo Family

This is one of the commonest, queerest and most spectacular of desert plants, especially when, after sufficient rains, the tips of its long, thorny branches seem afire with dense clusters of brilliant red blossoms. Often reaching a height of 20 feet, it is found in the Mohave and Colorado Deserts and in Arizona.

10. BLOSSOM OF THE OCOTILLO

11. MECCA ASTER
Aster cognatus
Sunflower Family
Flower lavender with yellow
center. A bushy plant, 1-2
feet tall, found at bases of
vertical walls in Painted and
Box Canyons growing in
sandstone and clay crevices.
Colorado Desert.

12. CHUPAROSA
Beloperone californica
Acanthus Family
Flower dull red. A low,
rounded shrub, found at low
altitudes along borders of
sandy washes and among rocks
of the Colorado Desert. Hum-
ming birds probe the blossoms
for both insects and nectar.

13. THISTLE SAGE
Salvia carduacea
Mint Family
Flower lavender, with red
anthers. Plant woolly, with
basal rosette of prickly leaves.
Colorado and Mohave Deserts.

14. MOHAVE OWL'S CLOVER
Orthocarpus purpurascens
ornatus
Figwort Family
Flower velvety-red to purple,
with the lower lip tipped with
yellow. Mohave Desert.

15. FRINGED ONION
Allium fimbriatum
Lily Family
Flower purple to pale rose,
with darker midvein, borne
on a stem 2 to 3 inches high.
The solitary leaf usually is
curled near the ground.
Colorado and Mohave Deserts.

16. BIGELOW MIMULUS
Mimulus Bigelovii
Figwort Family
A low-growing, branched annual
with reddish stems, thin leaves
and delicate reddish purple
flowers. Common in gravelly
or sandy washes and canyons,
on all three deserts.

17. CLEVELAND PENTSTEMON
Penstemon Clevelandii connatus
Figwort Family
Flower purplish-red, plant with several stems 16-30 inches high. Western edge of the Colorado Desert.

18. WHITE RATANY
Krameria Grayi
Pea Family
Flower red-purple. A low-branched shrub 1-2 feet high, parasitic on the roots of another woody plant with which it is associated. In May, masses of fragrant flowers appear on the stiff branches. Found on all three deserts.

19. HAIRY SAND-VERBENA
Abronia villosa
Four-o'Clock Family
Flower purplish-rose. A
trailing annual, partial to dunes
and sand flats. The clusters of
flowers make a fine show of
color and are very fragrant.
Common to all three deserts.

20. SUGAR-BUSH
Rhus ovata
Sumac Family
An evergreen shrub with stout
reddish twigs, leathery leaves
and small reddish flower buds
in dense clusters. In spring,
pinkish flowers open and are
followed by acid-covered
fruits. Common to the Colorado
and Mohave Deserts

21. BROAD-FLOWERED GILIA
Gilia latiflora
Phlox Family
Flower pink to violet, with
yellow throat. Mohave Desert.

22. HERON BILL - FILAREE
Erodium cicutarium
Geranium Family
A naturalized annual with
rose-violet flowers.
All three deserts.

23. FAIRY-DUSTER - MESQUITILLA
Calliandra eriophylla
Pea Family
Flower rose to reddish-purple, with long, white stamens tipped scarlet. A low densely-branched, thornless shrub with acacia-like leaves. On all three deserts.

24. GIANT FOUR-O'CLOCK
Mirabilis Froebelii
Four-o'Clock Family
Flowers purplish-red, opening in the afternoon. A perennial, often forming large round mats some 3-4 feet across. Found on the Colorado and Mohave Deserts.

25. PURPLE PRIMROSE
Oenothera heterochroma
Evening Primrose Family
Flower purple to red. A
spreading plant 8-15 inches
tall with hairy, glandular her-
bage, found in Death Valley
National Monument.

26. MANZANITA
Arctostaphylos
Heath Family
An erect, much-branched
shrub, 3-6 feet high, with
small, delicate pink flowers.
Found on dry slopes in the
Mohave Desert.

27. DESERT PHLOX
Phlox Stansburyi
Phlox Family
Flower pinkish-red to white.
A low-growing, woody-based
perennial found on dry,
gravelly slopes and washes
in all three deserts.

28. DESERT FIVESPOT CHINESE LANTERN
Malvastrum rotundifolium
Mallow Family
Flower rose-pink to lilac,
remaining globular, and with
a red spot on the inner base
of each petal. All three
deserts.

29. DESERT CALICO
Langloisia Matthewsii
Phlox Family
Flower whitish to pink,
with red and white markings.
A low, long-blooming spring
annual. Mohave Desert.

30. WILD RHUBARB
Rumex hymenosepalus
Buckwheat Family
Flower pinkish. A coarse,
herbaceous, somewhat
reddish perennial with
acid sap. Found on all
three deserts.

31. COLDENIA
Coldenia plicata
Borage Family
A perennial with prostrate, trailing stems and gray-green, deeply pleated leaves. Small, bluish-lavender flowers are inconspicuous. All three deserts.

32. DESERT IRONWOOD
Olneya tesota
Pea Family
A wide crowned tree bearing, usually in June, masses of violet-purple flowers. It grows in sandy canyons and washes in all three deserts below 2,000 feet.

33. JOINT FIR - SQUAW TEA
Ephedra
Joint Fir Family
A harsh, stringy perennial,
often several feet tall, bearing
leaves reduced to tiny scales.
It is sometimes harvested for
brewing "Squaw Tea", or
"Mormon Tea". Common
on all three deserts.

34. SPOTTED GILIA
LILAC SUNBONNET
Langloisia punctata
Phlox Family
Flowers violet, with purple
dots. A low, tufted, heavy-
blooming annual found on
the Mohave Desert.

35. PINK MARIPOSA LILY
Calochortus
Lily Family
One of many species of
Calochortus with flowers of
many colors, closely related
to the Sego Lily, State Flower
of Utah. Found on higher
elevations in the Colorado and
Mohave Deserts.

36. ROSE SAGE
Salvia pachyphylla
Mint Family
Flower blue, bracts purple.
A compact shrub often form-
ing low, broad round mats
3-4 feet in diameter. Not
common, but found on the
Colorado and Mohave Deserts.

37. PURPLE MAT
Nama demissum
Waterleaf Family
Flower purplish-red. A
small prostrate annual, common on flat clay and sandy
soils, in all three deserts.
With enough moisture, it
spreads over large areas,
while in dry seasons it may
bear only a single flower.

38. PAPER-BAG BUSH
Salazaria mexicana
Mint Family
Flower purple-white. A
rounded bush with many
inflated, papery pods which
in age often become tinged
with rose. It grows in
washes on rocky hillsides
in the Colorado and
Mohave Deserts.

39. CALTHA-LEAVED PHACELIA
Phacelia calthifolia
Waterleaf Family
Flower purple. A coarse-
stemmed annual, 4-12 inches
high, with sticky glands on the
herbage. Colorado and Mohave
Deserts.

40. ARROW-WEED
Pluchea sericea
Sunflower Family
Flowers pale purple, growing
in terminal clusters on the
branches. Willow-like leaves
are covered with silvery hairs.
Shrub grows erect to 12' in
dense stands on all three
deserts.

41. DESERT WILD PARSLEY
Lomatium mohavense
Carrot Family
Flower deep maroon. The leaves, fruit and stems are grayish, because of a dense covering of hairs. Found on the Mohave Desert.

42. ROCK GILIA
Gilia scopulorum
Phlox Family
Flower rose-lavender, with yellow throat. Colorado and Mohave Deserts.

43. YERBA SANTA
Eriodictyon trichocalyx lanatum
Waterleaf Family
Flower white to pale lavender. Erect shrub, 1½-4 feet tall with dark green leaves, sticky above, white and felty beneath. Canyons of the Colorado Desert.

44. CHOLLA CANE CACTUS
WALKING STICK CACTUS
Opuntia spinosior
Cactus Family
Flower red to purple. Fruit yellow. Arizona Desert.

45. MOHAVE LOCOWEED
Astragalus mohavensis
Pea Family
Flower rose-purple. Plant
grows on dry slopes and in
the valleys of the northern
and eastern Mohave Desert.

46. SPANISH NEEDLE
Palafoxia linearis
Sunflower Family
Flower deep pink. Annual,
1-2 feet high, with dark green,
exceedingly bitter herbage.
Plentiful along roadsides in
the spring. Found on sandy
flats, in the Colorado and
Mohave Deserts.

47. SCENTED PENTSTEMON
Penstemon Palmeri
Figwort Family
Flower rose-pink. This tall
plant, 2-5 feet, is found in
gravelly soil and washes of
the eastern Mohave Desert.

48. DESERT LAVENDER
Hyptis Emoryi
Mint Family
The small flowers are
violet-blue, two lipped.
An aromatic shrub, erect,
3-10 feet tall, with woolly
leaves. All three deserts.

49. ROTHROCK THISTLE
Cirsium rothrocki
Sunflower Family
Flower rose-colored to
carmine. Found on the
Arizona Desert.

50. SMOOTH-STEMMED FAGONIA
Fagonia chilensis laevis
Caltrop Family
Flower purple to crimson.
A low spiny, slightly shrubby
plant, with almost smooth
stems. Found on bare rocky
hills and basins of the Colorado Desert.

Notes

Notes

Notes

Notes

Blue Flowers
of the Desert

INDEX

Bluish Flowers

51. ROYAL DESERT LUPINE
Lupinus odoratus
Pea Family
Flowers bright blue or purple;
plant often forming a rosette
in the sand. Mohave and
Arizona Deserts.

52. GREAT BASIN BLUE SAGE
Salvia Dorrii
Mint Family
Flowers blue. Bracts and
calyces purplish. Mohave
and Arizona Deserts.

53. DAVY GILIA
Gilia Davyi
Phlox Family
Flower violet to pink, with yellow throat. A splendid, showy species, found in sandy soils of the Mohave Desert.

54. SMALL-LEAVED AMSONIA
Amsonia brevifolia
Dogbane Family
Flower bluish. A many-stemmed, perennial herb, with milky juice and stems 8-15 inches tall.
Found in the higher elevations of the Mohave and northern Colorado Deserts.

55. PURPLE NIGHTSHADE -
GROUNDCHERRY -
WILD POTATO
Solanum xanti
Potato Family
Flower purple. These common
roadside plants, quite showy
when in bloom, attract attention
during late spring and summer.
Common on all three deserts.

56. PARRY PHACELIA
Phacelia Parryi
Waterleaf Family
Flower royal purple or deep
violet. An erect annual with
handsome, shallow-cupped
flowers and hairy-glandular
herbage. Found on the
Colorado Desert.

57. SMOKE TREE
Dalea spinosa
Pea Family
Flower blue-purple. A thorny, almost leafless, gray-green shrub, up to 20 feet tall, growing in sandy washes, below 1,500 feet. Flowers in June-July. All three deserts.

58. INDIGO BUSH
MESA DALEA
Dalea Schottii
Pea Family
Flower indigo-blue. An intricately branched bush, 3 to 6 feet high, with bright green leaves. Colorado and Arizona Deserts.

59. BLUE-EYED GRASS
Sisyrinchium bellum
Iris Family
Flowers deep blue, with
yellow centers, borne at
the top of branching, flat-
tish stems about 12 inches
tall. Leaves basal and grass-
like. Confined on the desert
to alkaline seeps. Colorado
Desert.

60. DESERT DELPHINIUM -
LARKSPUR
Delphinium Parishii
Crowfoot Family
Flower varies from light to
deeper blue, and even to
pinkish-purple. The only
Desert Delphinium, it is
found on the Colorado and
Mohave Deserts.

61. CAMPANULATE PHACELIA - CANTERBURY BELLS
Phacelia campanularia
Waterleaf Family
Flowers royal purple, or deep blue. A loosely branching annual, 4 inches to 3 feet high, with broad leaves and somewhat bowl-shaped flowers. Found on the Colorado and Mohave Deserts below 4,000 feet.

62. BRISTLY GILIA
Gilia setosissima
Phlox Family
Flower light violet or pale blue. A low, tufted, freely flowering annual with long-lasting flowers. Common on dry sands of washes and mesas in the Colorado and Mohave Deserts.

63. SQUAW CABBAGE - DESERT CANDLE
Caulanthus inflatus
Mustard Family
Erect, usually unbranched annual with green and lemon-yellow, inflated stems 1-2 feet high, bearing many leaves below, purplish flowers above, and studded with purplish buds at the tip. Common, on open flats, above 2,000 feet in the Mohave Desert.

64. WILD HELIOTROPE
Phacelia
Waterleaf Family
Flower lavender or bluish. An annual 1-3 feet high, with fern-like leaves and coiled cymes of small flowers, often growing up through other plants. Found on all three deserts.

TELEPHONE MESSAGE

TO M _Cameron_ _____ ROOM _____

M _Eliz Bennett_

CALLED YOU UP

TIME _____ M   DATE _____

WILL CALL AGAIN _leaving tomorrow_

REQUEST THAT YOU CALL _back abt 1 : 8_

REMARKS _April —_

65. CHIA
Salvia Columbariae
Mint Family
Flower blue. An annual,
generally short, with leaves
mostly basal. Common in
all three deserts.

66. DESERT WILLOW -
DESERT CATALPA
Chilopsis linearis
Bignonia Family
Flower white to lavender
and pink. A shrubby tree,
6-15 feet, having willow-like
foliage and orchid-like, violet
scented flowers. These appear
after summer rains and are
followed by long, slender seed
pods which remain dangling
for long periods. Found in
washes below 5,000 feet on
the Colorado and Mohave
Deserts.

67. PINK-SPOTTED GILIA
Gilia maculata
Phlox Family
Flower white, with pink spots
on each corolla lobe. Grows
in sandy washes of the
Colorado Desert.

68. FREMONT PHACELIA
Phacelia Fremontii
Waterleaf Family
Flower lavender-violet, with
yellow throat. A common
annual of sandy stretches
and dry streamways of the
Mohave Desert.

69. ADONIS LUPINE
Lupinus excubitus
Pea Family
A handsome perennial,
with blue to lilac flowers.
Mohave Desert.

70. PRICKLY GILIA
Gilia pungens tenuiloba
Phlox Family
Flower bluish-white.
A low-growing perennial,
growing on rocky slopes
of all three deserts.

71. BABY BLUE-EYES
Nemophila Menziesii
Waterleaf Family
Flower dark to light blue, and
often dotted or veined with
purple. Slender succulent
annual on western edge of the
Colorado and Mohave Deserts.

Notes

Notes

Notes

Notes

White Flowers
of the Desert

INDEX

Whitish Flowers

72. FISHHOOK CACTUS
Mamillaria dioica
Cactus Family
Flower creamy, fruit scarlet.
Surface under the spines is
not ribbed, but consists of
small, rounded pyramids, with
a cluster of spines growing
from the top of each. In
sandy places below 2,000
feet in the Colorado Desert.

73. DESERT RANGE ALMOND
Prunus fasciculata
Rose Family
Flower white. A much-
branched, deciduous shrub,
growing about 8 feet tall.
Grows in clumps on rocky
slopes and in canyons of
the Colorado and Mohave
Deserts.

74. DESERT ALYSSUM
Lepidium Fremontii
Mustard Family
Flower white. A bushy, green-stemmed, rounded perennial, 1 - 2 feet tall, bearing many small, fragrant flowers. Common in rocky or sandy places below 5,000 feet, chiefly on the Mohave Desert.

75. DESERT WHITE ASTER
Aster Leucelene
Sunflower Family
Flower white. A low plant with woody base and glandular leaves, covered with stiffish hairs, growing in the eastern Mohave Desert.

76. DESERT APRICOT
Prunus Fremontii
Rose Family
Flower white. A rigidly
branched deciduous shrub with
twigs ending in thorns, and
with fragrant flowers ½ inch
across. In the western Colorado
Desert.

77. POPCORN FLOWER
Cryptantha
Borage Family
One of many desert species,
usually with prickly hairs
and flowers in coiled cymes.
All three deserts.

78. SULPHUR-THROATED FORGET-ME-NOT
Cryptantha flavoculata
Borage Family
Flower white, with yellow
throat. A perennial, with stems
4 - 10 inches tall and rounded
basal leaves. On the Mohave Desert.

79. WINTER FAT
Eurotia lanata
Pigweed Family
Flowers of two types: stami-
nate, consisting of a four-
parted calyx and four stamens;
pistillate, with the pistil between two connected bracts.
A shrub 1 - 3 feet tall with
white-woolly stellate hairs,
important for winter grazing.
Common, above 2,000 feet,
in the Mohave Desert.

80. DESERT LILY
Hesperocallis undulata
Lily Family
Flower white, with bluish-green band down the center of the back of each petal. At the base of the stem which may become several feet high are ruffle-edged, elongate blue-green leaves. It has wide distribution on dry, sandy flats below 2,000 feet in all three deserts.

81. DESERT CHICORY
Rafinesquia neomexicana
Sunflower Family
Ray-flowers white, veined rose-purple on the outer side. A weak-stemmed annual, common in the shade of shrubs and in canyons of the Colorado and Mohave Deserts.

82. FREMONT PINCUSHION
Chaenactis Fremontii
Sunflower Family
Flower white. A simple, erect or branching annual, with marginal flowers of the head often enlarged and irregular. A variable species, common in all three deserts.

83. DESERT TOBACCO
Nicotiana trigonophylla
Potato Family
Flower white. A viscid, usually perennial shrub 1-3 feet high. Found in low rocky canyons and washes on all three deserts.

84. SACRED DATURA
JIMSON WEED
Datura meteloides
Potato Family
Flowers white, with
purplish tinge. All
three deserts.

85. PRICKLY POPPY
Argemone corymbosa
Poppy Family
Flowers white and crinkly.
A spiny perennial, 2 to 3
feet tall. Mohave Desert.

86. BOTTLE WASHER
Oenothera decorticans
Evening Primrose Family
Flower white, fading to pink.
A stout annual with thick
stem and woody capsules.
Found on the Colorado and
Mohave Deserts.

87. SPECTACLE-POD
Dithyrea californica
Mustard Family
Flower white. An annual
with coarsely toothed leaves
and spreading stems ending
in racemes of flowers. Pods,
deeply notched above and
below, look like a pair of
spectacles. Common on all
three deserts.

88. PARRY GILIA
Gilia Parryae
Phlox Family
Flower white, with variations
to bluish purple. A low much-
branched little annual, sometimes almost covering sandy
places with white. Found
on the Mohave Desert.

89. DESERT STAR
Monoptilon bellioides
Sunflower Family
Flower white, to pinkish, with
yellow center. A low growing,
daisy-like little annual, abundant in sandy or stony places
below 3,000 feet on all three
deserts.

90. WHITE TIDY TIPS
Layia glandulosa
Sunflower Family
Flower white or pinkish, with orange center. A glandular annual, 1-2 feet high, with leaves and stems covered with short, stiff hairs. Common in loose, sandy soils below 3,000 feet. Found on the Colorado and Mohave Deserts.

91. SAND MAT
Euphorbia polycarpa
Spurge Family
A low, milky-juiced perennial spreading over sandy places below 4,000 feet in all three deserts.

92. ROCK DAISY
Perityle Emoryi
Sunflower Family
Flower, white rays, yellow
center. A freely branching
annual, ½-2 feet tall, with
brittle, succulent stems.
Common in rock crevices
and canyons below 3,000
feet in the Colorado and
Mohave Deserts.

93. WHITE TACK-STEM
Calycoseris Wrightii
Sunflower Family
Rays white, with rose or
purplish dots on the back.
An annual, with tack-shaped
glands on the upper parts
of the stems. Colorado
and Mohave Deserts.

94. CHEESE BUSH
Hymenoclea Salsola
Sunflower Family
Flowers unisexual. Pistillate
flowers surrounded by silvery
to reddish scales. Plant 2-3
feet high, common in sandy
washes of the Colorado and
Mohave Deserts.

95. SAHUARO
GIANT CACTUS
Carnegiea gigantea
Cactus Family
Flower creamy-white.
This largest of the U.S. Cacti
is the State Flower of Arizona.
A few plants grow on the
eastern border of the
Colorado Desert.

96. DUNE PRIMROSE
Oenothera deltoides
Evening Primrose Family
Flower white, turning to pink.
A large flowered, sweet-scented plant common in sandy areas below 3,500 feet.
Outer stems, in aging turn inward and upward, forming "baskets" or "bird cages".
Found on the Colorado and Mohave Deserts

97. WHIPPLE YUCCA
Yucca Whipplei
Lily Family
Flowers waxy white. Sometimes called "Our Lord's Candle". The plant, with its clumps of stiff, sword-like leaves and tall stalks bearing masses of creamy-white flowers is common in the coastal sides of mountains bordering the desert, but is rare on the eastern slopes. It is protected by law.

98. CLIFF ROSE
Cowania Stansburiana
Rose Family
Flower cream-white. A bush
3-8 feet high, with gland-dot-
ted leaves and solitary flowers
at the ends of short branches.
It grows on dry slopes and in
canyons of the Mohave and
Arizona Deserts.

99. NOLINA
Nolina Bigelovii
Lily Family
Flower whitish. Leaves
rather narrow, flat and
smooth-margined.
Colorado Desert.

100. JOSHUA TREE - TREE YUCCA
Yucca brevifolia
Lily Family
Flower greenish-white to ivory. A sturdy tree growing 20-30 feet tall with many branches and clusters of sharp, spine-like leaves. Flowers in tight groups at the ends of branches, do not open wide. Blooming depends on temperature and moisture and does not occur every year. On the Mohave and Arizona Deserts.

101. MOHAVE YUCCA
Yucca schidigera
Lily Family
Flowers cream with purplish tinge. The most common yucca of all three deserts, with long, yellow-green, trough-like leaves with curling fibers on the margins.

102. APACHE PLUME
Fallugia paradoxa
Rose Family
Flower white. It is a small
bush, seldom more than 3
feet in height. Used sometimes as an erosion control
plant. Mohave and
Arizona Deserts.

103. DESERT MILKWEED
Asclepias erosa
Milkweed Family
Flower greenish-white. A
perennial, with stems 2-5
feet tall and broad leaves in
pairs. Flowers are in clusters,
and the capsules contain
many flat seeds each with a
tuft of white hairs. Common
on all three deserts, below
5,000 feet.

104. DESERT HOLLY
Atriplex hymenelytra
Pigweed Family
A low rounded shrub grow-
ing in dry, alkaline places in
all three deserts. The female
plants bear large, light green,
disc-shaped fruiting bracts.
Leaves are silvery and often
used for Christmas decorations.

105. DEATH VALLEY LOCOWEED
Astragalus funereus
Pea Family
Lower parts of flowers
white, upper parts tipped
with bluish-violet. A low
plant, with strong, tuberous
root. Mohave Desert.

106. CALIFORNIA CHICORY
Rafinesquia californica
Sunflower Family
A stout-branched annual with
white flowers. Found on all
three deserts.

107. CLIFF ASTER
Malacothrix saxatilis
Sunflower Family
Flower white, occasionally
with purple ends to rays.
Plant grows 1-3½ feet tall
on rocky soils or clay hills
of the Colorado and Mohave
Deserts.

108. WAND SAGE
Salvia Vaseyi
Mint Family
Flower white, on tall,
wand-like branches.
Colorado and Mohave
Deserts.

109. SANDPAPER PLANT
Petalonyx Thurberi
Loasa Family
Flower white. A fragrant-
flowered perennial with woody
base, and surface of stem and
leaves covered with short,
barbed hairs. All three
deserts.

110. ANNUAL MITRA
Stephanomeria exigua
Sunflower Family
White to reddish ray
flowers often turn
yellow in age. All
three deserts.

111. WILD BUCKWHEAT
Eriogonum
Buckwheat Family
A shrub with tall stems,
grayish leaves and small,
white flowers. All three
deserts.

112. TEDDY BEAR CHOLLA CACTUS
Opuntia Bigelovii
Cactus Family
Flower yellow-green to white.
An erect plant, usually with
a single trunk, topped with
short, lateral branches crowd-
ed with straw-colored, retrosely
barbed spines. Common to all
three deserts.

113. FLEABANE SPREADING DAISY
Erigeron divergens
Sunflower Family
Flower white to lavender.
All three deserts.

Notes

Notes

Notes

Notes

Yellow Flowers
of the Desert

INDEX

Yellowish Flowers

114. LARGE YELLOW DESERT PRIMROSE
Oenothera primiveris
Evening Primrose Family
Flower lemon-yellow, aging
to orange-red. A low annual
with long taproot, a rosette
of leaves and flower stem 1-3
inches high. On sandy soil of
the Colorado and Mohave
Deserts.

115. WOOLLY MARIGOLD
Baileya pleniradiata
Sunflower Family
Flower yellow. An annual
with grayish foliage and leafy
stems 4 inches to 2 feet high.
Wide spread in all three
deserts, on sandy flats and
along roadsides.

116. BROWN-EYED PRIMROSE - PETITE PRIMROSE
Oenothera
Evening Primrose Family
Flower white to pale yellow.
Commonly found on the Colorado
Desert, but sometimes on the
Mohave.

117. DESERT CASSIA
Cassia armata
Pea Family
A many-branched shrub
with sweet scented, yellow
flowers, growing 3-4 feet tall,
often called Desert Senna.
All three deserts.

118. MOHAVE PRICKLY PEAR
Opuntia mohavensis
Cactus Family
Flower pale yellow to orange.
Found on the Mohave Desert
between 3,000 and 5,000 feet.

119. DESERT GOLD POPPY
Eschscholtzia glyptosperma
Poppy Family
Flowers bright yellow, on
numerous erect stems.
Mohave Desert.

120. YELLOW CUPS
Oenothera brevipes
Evening Primrose Family
Flowers brilliant yellow.
A free-flowering annual
with mostly basal leaves
in a rosette, and reddish
stems up to 15 inches
high. Common on stony
hills and dry flats in the
Colorado and Mohave
Deserts.

121. GOLDEN GILIA
Gilia aurea
Phlox Family
Flower yellow, with brownish
throat. A low, several-
branched plant, common in
sandy areas below 6,000 feet
in the Colorado and Mohave
Deserts.

122. VENUS BLAZING STAR
Mentzelia nitens
Loasa Family
Flower yellow, stem white.
Common on sandy or gravelly
soil in all three deserts.

123. CLIMBING MILKWEED
Sarcostemma hirtellum
Milkweed Family
Flowers greenish-yellow. A
slender-stemmed, twining
plant with milky sap. All
three deserts.

124. GOLDEN CHOLLA CACTUS
Opuntia echinocarpa
Cactus Family
Flower yellow, tinged with red. An intricately branched plant, 2-5 feet high with many straw-colored spines. Common in all three deserts.

125. CALIFORNIA DODDER
Cuscuta californica
Morning Glory Family
A parasite on several plants, e.g. burro bush and creosote bush, common in the Colorado and Mohave Deserts.

126. YELLOW TURBAN
Eriogonum pusillum
Buckwheat Family
Flowers bright yellow to
reddish. An annual 4-12
inches high, the leaves
somewhat greenish above
but white-felty beneath.
Found in the Colorado
and Mohave Deserts.

127. GOLDENHEAD
*Acamptopappus
sphaerocephalus*
Sunflower Family
A small shrub, with
many, almost leafless,
whitish stems, bearing
small, pale yellow flower
heads. All three deserts.

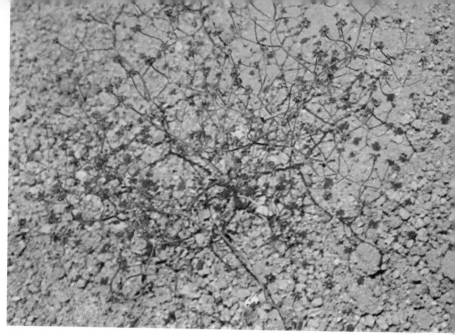

128. MOUNTAIN MIST
Eriogonum Parishii
Buckwheat Family
Plant suggests a fine
greenish or reddish mist
with its tiny flowers and
numerous slender branches.
Mohave Desert.

129. DEERHORN CACTUS
Opuntia acanthocarpa
Cactus Family
Flower yellow, greenish-
yellow to red. A much-
branched cane cactus, with
spiny fruits and straw-colored
spines. All three deserts.

130. BIGELOW COREOPSIS
Coreopsis Bigelovii
Sunflower Family
Flower yellow. An annual with
naked stems and basal leaves.
Found on dry flats in the
Colorado and Mohave Deserts.

131. YELLOW SAUCERS
Malocothrix sonchoides
Sunflower Family
An annual, 4-12 inches tall,
with fragrant yellow flowers.
Common in the Mohave Desert
in sandy areas, from 2,000 feet
to 5,000 feet.

132. SCREW BEAN
MESQUITE - TORNILLA
Prosopis pubescens
Pea Family
Flower yellow, consisting
largely of a tuft of stamens.
A deciduous shrub or small
tree, sometimes 20 feet tall,
usually growing in thickets
in sandy or loamy soil near
water. Tightly-coiled seed
pods give the plant its name.
In the Colorado and Mohave
Deserts.

133. DESERT DANDELION
Malacothrix glabrata
Sunflower Family
Flower pale yellow, often with
a small, bright-red "button" in
the center. A many stemmed
annual, abundant on sandy
areas in all three deserts.

134. SAND BLAZING STAR
Mentzelia involucrata
Loasa Family
Flower pale cream, with crimson-tinged center. An annual, branching from the base, with stiff hairs. Found in low hot washes and on canyon sides on all three deserts.

135. DESERT VELVET - VELVET ROSETTE
Psathyrotes ramosissima
Sunflower Family
Flower yellow. A low, rounded plant with conspicuous, gray-green, velvety leaves. Found on dry, hard soil in all three deserts.

136. COYOTE MELON - PALMATE - LEAVED GOURD
Cucurbita palmata
Gourd Family
Flower yellow. A plant with trailing stems 4-6 feet long, spreading radially on the sands. Colorado and Mohave Deserts.

137. GOAT-NUT, JOJOBA
Simmondsia chinensis
Box Family
Flower greenish-yellow. A leathery-leaved, stiff-branched shrub, up to 6 feet tall. Male and female flowers are borne separately. Common on dry slopes below 5,000 feet on all three deserts.

138. PRINCE'S PLUME - DESERT PLUME
Stanleya pinnata
Mustard Family
Flower yellow. A woody-based plant, growing 2-5 feet tall, with several stems bearing terminal racemes. Found largely in selenium-bearing soil of washes and slopes in the Mohave Desert.

139. DESERT WALLFLOWER
Erysimum asperum
Mustard Family
Flower yellow. Plants often grow up through shrubs. Mohave Desert.

140. CAT'S CLAW
Acacia Greggii
Pea Family
Flowers yellow, small, fragrant,
in cylindrical spikes, each with
similar petals and many stamens.
A spreading deciduous shrub
with short, recurved spines.
Found in washes and canyons,
below 6,000 feet in all three
deserts.

141. FIDDLENECK
Amsinckia tessellata
Borage Family
Flower orange-yellow. A
plant with stiff prickly hairs
and coiled flower clusters.
Colorado and Mohave
Deserts.

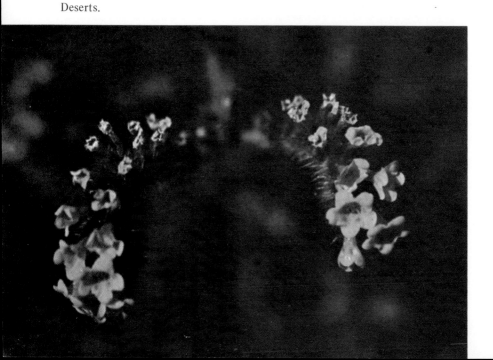

142. ERIOPHYLLUM
Eriophyllum Wallacei
Sunflower Family
Flower yellow. A low woolly annual, frequent on sandy and gravelly flats of all three deserts.

143. DESERT AGAVE
Agave deserti
Amaryllis Family
Flower yellow. Plant with flower stalk 15 or more feet tall, with thick, succulent leaves, usually growing in colonies. Found on the Colorado and Mohave Deserts.

144. BARREL CACTUS - BISNAGA

Echinocactus acanthodes
Cactus Family
Flower greenish-yellow.
Plant is first globular in form,
but becomes cylindrical and
may grow to a height of
several feet. Spines, usually
curved and white or rose-
colored, are borne on stout
ribs. Common in all three
deserts.

145. GRIZZLY-BEAR CACTUS

Opuntia ursina
Cactus Family
Flower yellow. Plants
covered with flexible
ashy-gray spines, some-
times 8 inches long.
Mohave Desert.

146. CREOSOTE BUSH - GREASE-WOOD
Larrea divaricata
Caltrop Family
Flower yellow, with twisted petals. Plant has waxy, green leaves and blackish stems and grows 3-12 feet tall. Fruit, covered with white hairs, is almost as noticeable as the flowers. Dominant plant on all three deserts.

147. YELLOW TACKSTEM
Calycoseris Parryi
Sunflower Family
Flower yellow-white. Plant growing from 4 inches to 2 feet high, with dark, tack-shaped glands on the stems, in sandy soils of the Colorado and Mohave Deserts.

148. PAPER FLOWER
Psilostrophe Cooperi
Sunflower Family
Flowers deep yellow, persisting on the stem till they become dry and papery. A woody-based, many-stemmed shrub, common on rocky mesas and fans in all three deserts.

149. BLADDER POD
Isomeris arborea
Caper Family
Flower yellow. A much-branched, ill-scented shrub growing several feet high and blooming much of the year. Abundant on the Colorado and Mohave Deserts.

150. GOLDEN MARIPOSA LILY
Calochortus Nuttallii aureus
Lily Family
Flower bright yellow. Found in higher altitudes on all three deserts.

151. DESERT ZYGADENE
Zygadenus brevibracteatus
Lily Family
Flowers yellowish
A bulbous plant with flower stalk 1 to 2 feet tall.
Mohave Desert.

152. TOOTH-LEAVED PRIMROSE
Oenothera dentata
Evening Primrose Family
A dainty plant with slender
branches and yellow flowers.
Mohave Desert.

153. CHINCH-WEED
Pectis papposa
Sunflower Family
Flower bright yellow with very
green, narrow leaves. A heavily
scented, low annual, often after
summer rains, carpeting sand
and clay flats of the Colorado
and Mohave Deserts.

154. TREE POPPY
Dendromecon rigida
Poppy Family
Flower bright yellow. A shrub
2-8 feet tall, with stiff, leathery,
willow-shaped leaves. Found
on the brush slopes of the
Mohave Desert.

155. ENCELIA - BRITTLE-BUSH - INCIENSO
Encelia farinosa
Sunflower Family
Flowers with yellow rays and
yellow or brown centers. A
compact, dome-shaped bush,
with silvery-gray leaves and
woody trunk and stems which
exude crystals of resin. Common on rocky slopes and in
washes of all three deserts.

156. SPENCER PRIMROSE
Oenothera micrantha exfoliata
Evening Primrose Family
Flower lemon-yellow. A
low-growing annual, common
to all three deserts.

157. TIDY-TIPS
Layia platyglossa
Sunflower Family
Flower bright yellow, with
white tipped rays. A gland-
ular annual, 1-2 feet high.
Common in sandy areas
in the Mohave Desert.

158. YELLOW COMET
Mentzelia affinis
Loasa Family
Flower bronzy-yellow. An
annual 8 inches to 2 feet
high, with rather thick,
white, shining stems and
many flowers, found in
all three deserts.

**159. SALMON-FLOWERED
PRICKLY PEAR**
Opuntia Vaseyi
Cactus Family
Stems are flattened joints
covered with spines and
glochids. Colorado Desert.

160. HAIRY LOTUS
Lotus tomentellus
Pea Family
Flower yellow, often reddish on back. An annual, growing over much of the three deserts.

161. LESSER MOHAVEA
Mohavea breviflora
Figwort Family
Flower bright yellow. An early spring annual, 2-6 inches high. Flower has three abortive and two fertile stamens. Plant grows in sandy or gravelly areas below 3,000 feet in the Mohave Desert.

162. GHOST FLOWER
Mohavea confertiflora
Figwort Family
Flower cream with purple
dots. An erect viscid annual
3-15 inches high, simple or
branched. Common in the
Colorado and Mohave
Deserts.

163. DARNING-NEEDLE
CACTUS - PENCIL CACTUS
Opuntia ramosissima
Cactus Family
Flower color variable,
greenish-yellow to brown.
A bushy shrub with slender,
usually spiny, stems. All
three deserts.

164. FOXTAIL CACTUS
Mamillaria Alversonii
Cactus Family
Flower purplish-yellow,
outer segments margined with
hairs. The short, cylindrical
stem has whitish spine
clusters. On the Mohave
Desert.

165. SCALE BUD
Anisocoma acaulis
Sunflower Family
Flower pale yellow. A
low, free-flowering annual,
with one-headed stems surrounded by a rosette of
toothed leaves. Found on
sandy flats and washes of
all three deserts.

166. KEYSIA
Glyptopleura setulosa
Sunflower Family
Flower creamy-yellow.
A sweet-scented annual,
whose light green leaves
with narrow white margins
are almost covered by
blossoms during spring
flowering. Found in
sandy areas of the Mohave
Desert.

167. CREAM CUP
Platystemon californicus crinitus
Poppy Family
An annual with slender,
hairy stems growing from
the base, and bearing single,
pale yellow flowers.
Colorado and Mohave Deserts.

**168. SALT BUSH
WINGSCALE**
Atriplex canescens
Pigweed Family
An erect, many-branched
shrub found on all three
deserts.

169. FREMONT XERASID
Syntrichopappus Fremontii
Sunflower Family
Flower golden yellow. A
woolly annual, not over 6
inches high, common in sandy
places on the Mohave Desert.

170. COTTON THORN
Tetradymia axillaris
Sunflower Family
A rigidly branched shrub with
slender spines and clear yellow
flowers. The fruit is covered
with white, woolly tufts, making
the plant seem covered with
cotton. Mohave Desert.

171. FREMONTIA
FLANNEL BUSH
Fremontia californica
Cacao Family
A showy shrub with clear
yellow flowers. Mohave
Desert.

172. PALMER BEAD POD
Lesquerella Palmeri
Mustard Family
An annual with slender
stems, small, bright
yellow flowers and round
fruits. All three deserts.

173. YELLOW-HEADS
Trichoptilium incisum
Sunflower Family
Flower bright yellow. A
low-growing annual, with
solitary heads on slender,
reddish stems. Found on
all three deserts.

174. MESCAT-ACACIA
Acacia constricta
Pea Family
A shrub with fragrant,
yellow blossoms, sometimes
called "white-thorn" because
of its long, slender, white
spines. Arizona Desert.

175. HONEY MESQUITE
Prosopis juliflora
Pea Family
Flowers yellow, minute and
arranged in spikes. A many-
branched shrub or tree, sometimes 15-20 feet tall, often almost buried under sand. The
sweetmeated pods ripen in
September or October and are
eaten by numerous mammals.
Common on all three deserts.

176. SUNFLOWER
Helianthus
Sunflower Family
A desert representative of
the familiar Compositae.

177. BORDER PALO VERDE
Cercidium floridum
Pea Family
A tree 12-20 feet high, with
blue-green bark and slender
branchlets, leafless much of
the year. Flowers, from March
to May, are yellow and numerous. A drought-resistant
plant, it is abundant in washes
and low, sandy areas on the
Colorado and Arizona Deserts.

178. DESERT TRUMPET
Eriogonum inflatum
Buckwheat Family
Flower yellow, minute. A perennial, with silvery, basal leaves and inflated stems, sometimes over 2 feet high, with thread-like branches. Common, below 6,000 feet, in rocky places on all three deserts.

179. PARRY NOLINA
Nolina Parryi
Lily Family
Flower creamy. Yellowish, dry-winged fruits often remain on the stalk for long periods. Colorado and Mohave Deserts.

**180. TWIN-FRUIT -
SMOOTH MENODORA**
Menodora spinescens
Olive Family
Flower yellow. A low,
spiny-branched shrub.
Mohave Desert.

181. MOHAVE THISTLE
Cirsium mohavense
Sunflower Family
Flower yellowish-white. A
tall biennial of the Mohave
Desert.

182. AJAMETE
Asclepias subulata
Milkweed Family
Flower greenish-yellow. A
perennial with many, almost
leafless stems 2-5 feet tall,
growing in hot, low areas of
all three deserts.

183. BUSH MONKEY FLOWER
Mimulus longiflorus
Figwort Family
Flower yellow or salmon. A
shrubby plant, 2-3 feet tall,
on the rocky, higher altitudes
of the Mohave Desert.

184. DESERT PINCUSHION
Coryphantha deserti
Cactus Family
A solitary form, with
straight, whitish spines.
Flower color varies from
straw-colored to pink.
Mohave Desert.

185. MUNZ CHOLLA CACTUS
Opuntia Munzii
Cactus Family
Flower yellowish-green, tinged
with red. Probably a hybrid
species, becoming tall and
shaggy in age. In canyons of
the Mohave Desert.

186. SMALL-LEAVED HOFFMANNSEGGIA

Hoffmannseggia microphylla
Pea Family
Flower yellow to orange-red.
This is a perennial shrub,
with several to many rush-
like stems 2-4 feet long.
Common in barren, stony
soils of the hills and canyons
of the Colorado and Arizona
Deserts.

187. WILD MARIGOLD

Baileya multiradiata
Sunflower Family
A woolly plant with leaves
mostly basal and tall stems,
each with a single yellow
flower head. Mohave Desert.

188. SAND-WASH GROUNDSEL
Senecio Douglasii
Sunflower Family
Flower yellow. A long-blooming, almost shrubby Senecio, common to sandy washes of all three deserts.

189. BURROBUSH
Franseria dumosa
Sunflower Family
A low, rounded, white-barked shrub, very common in the broad desert basins. Only during the spring season are the plants green. The flowers are of separate sexes. On all three deserts.

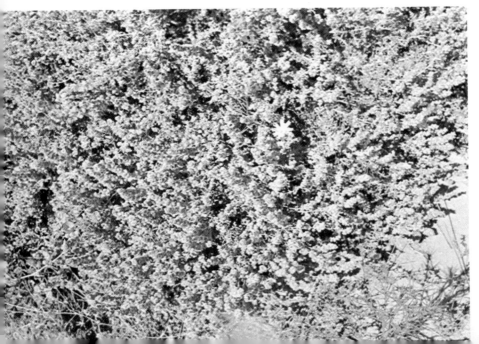

**190. YELLOW NIGHT-SHADE
GROUND-CHERRY**
Physalis crassifolia
Potato Family
A common perennial of
all three deserts.

The pictures presented in this book are
but a small sample of desert beauty:

*"Full many a flower is born
to blush unseen,
And waste its sweetness
on the desert air."*

Notes

Notes

Notes

Notes

References

ABRAMS, Leroy: *Illustrated Flora of the Pacific States.*

BENSON, Lyman S.: *Cacti of Arizona.*

CLEMENTS, Edith S.: *Flowers of Coast and Sierra.*

DAWSON, E. Yale: *Cacti of California.*

DODGE, Natt N.: *100 Desert Wildfolowers in natural color.*

DODGE, Natt N.: *Flowers of the Southwest Deserts.*

JAEGER, Edmund C.: *Desert Wild Flowers.*

JEPSON, W. L.: *Manual of the Flowering Plants of California.*

MUNZ, Philip A.: *California Desert Wildflowers.*

MUNZ, Philip A.: *California Spring Wildflowers.*

PARSONS, Mary Elizabeth: *The Wild Flowers of California.*

PATRAW, Pauline M.: *Flowers of the Southwest Mesas.*

RAVEN, Peter H.: *Native Shrubs of Southern California.*

Reported Uses of Desert Plants
by Desert Dwellers

3. **Beavertail Cactus:** One of the succulent plants, all parts of which - pods, flower buds, young fruit and seeds - were used for food by the desert Indians.

9. **Ocotillo:** Indians eat both flowers and seed. The bark contains resin and wax and makes a very hot fire.

26. **Manzanita:** The early settlers used the berries for making vinegar, brandy and jelly. Bears are fond of the berries, and the Indians eat them raw, or pound them into a meal from which a mush is made.

33. **Squaw Tea:** The Indians and early settlers boiled the stems to make a tea. Today, many desert dwellers enjoy a tea made from the stems.

40. **Arrow-weed:** Its straight stems were used by the Indians for arrow shafts, and for the construction of baskets and snares.

43. **Yerba Santa:** A tea made from the leaves was used as a cough remedy.

55. **Purple Nightshade:** Indians crushed the berries and added the juice to milk in making cheese.

63. **Squaw Cabbage:** Early settlers and Indians made a very satisfactory stew by boiling the young stems with meat.

65. **Chia:** Desert Indians used the seeds for food.

79. **Winter Fat:** Valuable winter grazing for sheep and cattle. The fresh roots are chewed and used as a remedy for burns by some desert Indians.

80. **Desert Lily:** Desert Indians and early settlers used the bulbs for flavoring food, as did Mexicans, who called it Ajo, their word for garlic.

83. **Desert Tobacco:** Indians used the leaves for smoking.

84. **Sacred Datura:** Desert Indians bruised and boiled the roots to make a drink which had a stupefying effect.

85. **Prickly Poppy:** The seeds are reported to be more narcotic than opium.

95. **Sahuaro Cactus:** Fruit is eaten, raw or cooked, or rolled into balls and dried. Syrup is fermented to make an intoxicant, and the oily seeds are ground into a paste to make a spread like butter.

98. **Cliff Rose:** A valuable browse plant for sheep, deer and cattle. Indians made cloth, mats and sandals from the silky inner bark.

103. **Desert Holly:** Used widely for Christmas decorations. It is disappearing from some parts of the desert, due to unrestrained picking by people.

132. **Screwbean Mesquite:** The pods are eaten by grazing animals. Indians eat the raw pods, and crush the ripe ones into a meal from which they make cakes.

137. **Goat-nut:** The nuts, rich in oil, were an important article of food among the Indians.

138. **Prince's Plume:** Young leaves were sometimes used as greens by Indians, after the first water in which they were boiled, apparently containing a residue of selenium from the soil, had been drained off, and cooking finished in fresh water.

140. **Cat's Claw:** Some Indians used the seeds as food, and also used a gum which exudes from the bark.

143. **Desert Agave:** The young sprouts, resembling asparagus shoots, but much larger, were roasted and much enjoyed by the Indians. From the leaf fibers, they made ropes and crude cloth.

153. **Chinch Weed:** This was used by the Indians for seasoning stews.

155. **Encelia:** The early Padres used the resin, which exuded from the stems, as incense. The Indians chewed the resin and smeared it on the body to relieve pain.

168. **Salt Bush:** Valuable for grazing. Desert Indians used the seeds for food.

177. **Border Paloverde:** The seeds were a source of food for the Indians.

178. **Desert Trumpet:** The tender tips of the stems are often used in salads.

182. **Ajamete:** The sap contains rubber, and is a possible future source of supply.

184. **Desert Pincushion:** Seeds were used for food by the Indians.

189. **Burrobush:** A preferred food for sheep and donkeys.